TRANSLATOR'S BLUES

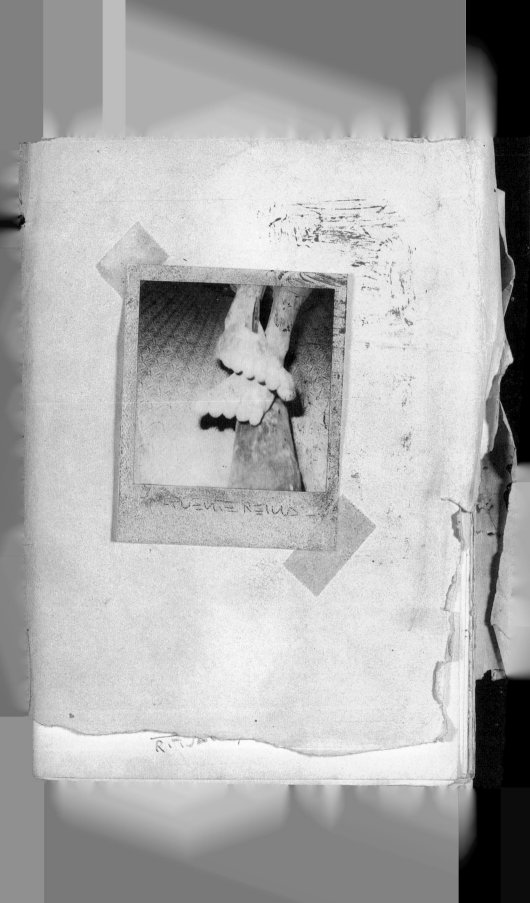

FRANCO NASI

Translator's Blues

Translated from the Italian by Dan Gunn

The Cahiers Series

CENTER FOR WRITERS & TRANSLATORS
THE AMERICAN UNIVERSITY OF PARIS

—

SYLPH EDITIONS

OVER THE COURSE OF MY LIFE, I've travelled a lot in the province of Reggio Emilia, where I was born and where, I expect, I'll die. My favourite time is the early morning during the summer, when normally one should be heading to work or on holiday: it's then I like to get on my bike and ride into the Apennines. When I reach a certain height I can sometimes catch a view of mountain ranges fading into the distance. Whenever this happens, when the sun has not yet picked out the colours and the mist is shrouding everything, Puccini's 'Nessun dorma' floats into my mind. Since I'm cycling alone, as always, and am fired up by Puccini's aria, I imagine myself the leader in one of those break-aways that happen in the Tour de France, the sort that so excite the journalists and readers of the sports pages. I begin to pedal as if pursued by a pack of wolves. But after a while the music has to end, and, since the mind is so busy remembering to oxygenate the blood, it has little left to spare for the Puccini aria. Then the pedals rotate more slowly, as before.

From a bicycle all the flaws in the asphalt become visible, the dents in the guard-rail, the rust on the road-signs, the ivy-covered acacias, the memorial stones with their dried flowers commemo-rating where a motorcyclist missed a corner, the steles with their plastic flowers dedicated to those who lost their lives liberating the Gothic Line, and the big round plaster Parmesan cheese indicating the little local Parmesan factory. Here I am, passing through a village with its bell tower, its bar, its bank-machine, and its news-stand in front of which are sandwich-boards displaying the local news headlines: on Sundays and Mondays car crashes; on Tuesdays and Wednesdays robberies from banks or villas; on Thursdays and Fridays updates on how the provincial bank is faring on the stock-market; on Saturdays the exodus towards the seaside. Not far from the village centre, I pass in front of an ochre-coloured enclosure wall, two large cement pine-cones placed atop the gate-posts, some cypresses, a generous parking-lot, black rails for securing bicycles: it's the country cemetery where, as people say, the dead fare better than their counterparts in the cramped and anonymous graveyards of the metropolis.

If you read the newspapers, you can well understand why everyone's busy erecting fences round their homes and installing remote-controlled gates and alarms. But I've often wondered why there's a need to build such solid walls round cemeteries; until, that is, I read a short text by a writer who is from my region but has spent a lot of time abroad, a writer who therefore sees things a bit differently, Daniele Benati: 'There are people saying incomprehensible things,' he writes, 'and others doing inexplicable things. Like Mauro Barchi, who had been buried in the cemetery in the morning but in the evening was already on his way to the bar.' Elsewhere, this same author tells of a football match played by the dead: a tricky event when staged by individuals who by right ought to be resting in silence. Tricky also for anyone wishing to have a kick at a ball, given that these days it's virtually impossible to find the space to play, ever since a fitness mania took hold, one that lasts well into old age. It's more and more common to see players, on the pitches in our region, hobbling after the ball, making you wonder if they're getting on in years, or if they're actually cadavers stretching their legs. For the good of all, then, it's appropriate that there be walls round the cemeteries, and that they be built high and solid.

It's also just as well that the tombs be located in rather out-of-the-way places and not on the main roads as used to be the case in Roman times, when along the Via Appia could be found monuments with epitaphs such as the following:

Wayfarer, brief is my message, halt and read!
This odious stone covers a beautiful woman.

I am the famous Scorpo, glory of the noisy circus,
object for a brief time, oh Rome, of your praise and happiness,
because the envious Lachesi Park
counting my victories and considering me an old man
snatched me at 27 years of age

The obvious thing to do, when confronted with such inscriptions, is to stop to meditate on the usefulness (or uselessness) of a woman's youthful beauty, or of chariot-race victories. There used to be less traffic, of course. Today it would be odd to see someone braking in front of a monument on the Via Emilia and being lured into meditation (inevitably provoking a traffic jam that would waste the time of those important people who have little time to waste).

In the provinces, architects do their utmost, therefore, to quarantine their cemeteries, so that anyone really wishing to reflect on death needs to push on through the gate (without first disturbing the traffic). They go to great lengths to create an orderly atmosphere, in which the dead can feel comfortable and overcome their wish to flee the place. And they do their utmost to satisfy even those customers who are seeking to confirm that they were once very well off. So it is that within the city of the dead there are tombs of wealthy families that resemble the little villas of residential neighbourhoods, featuring great displays of marble, small wrought-iron gates, and symbolic sculptures. Of course, there are also simple tombs, on the ground, belonging to those who could rise to no better. And then, in the surrounding suburbs, there are condominiums several storeys high, where everyone owns his own bedsit (or niche), these making up the most crowded neighbourhood of the necropolis.

There was a time when, after someone died, the men would put a black button in their buttonholes, and widows would wear weeds; in some parts, women were paid to lament; in others, big festas would take place with jazz bands trundling round the town on a cart. Whereas today, here in our province at least, we make believe that nothing at all has happened, and at funerals, people seem to cry less and less (the less one cries, the more one appears civilised and modern). It occurs to me that in the not-too-distant future funerals will be abolished altogether: a simulacrum is all that will remain, enacted on the Day of the Dead, run by the local authorities, with amateur actors accompanying an empty coffin to the graveyard, a pantomime priest leading the procession, play-acting choirboys, imitation holy water, incense, and band, just to show off to primary-school children the costumes of yesteryear.

"Noreta"

PRINCIPIO

The dead, the truly dead (if there still are any), will be sent promptly to their burial niches by the hygiene service working in collaboration with fast-delivery private companies, so as to avoid infections, fake whimpering, and loss of time (since time is coming to an end for one and all, and there is therefore no time to lose).

Epitaphs on tombs have already become a rarity. And since things that are rare are worth collecting, sometimes, when on my bicycle trips, I visit the cemeteries and jot down one or two in a green notebook, divided for the purpose into various sections according to the typology of the epitaph. There are those in which the defunct one speaks in the first person:

Nato lontano sono finito qui	Born afar I ended here
Passalacqua Battista	Passalacqua Battista
m. 22 marzo 1932	d. 22 March 1932

There are those where it's the parents speaking about the defunct:

In memoria di Giordani Bruno	In memory of Giordani Bruno
Morì giovane d'anni	Dead so young
e di meriti pieno	and so full of merit
Il mattino del 9	On the morning of 9
dicembre 1926	December 1926
Lacrimato dai suoi cari	Wept over by his dear parents
Compianto da tutti	Lamented by all

Then there are those that are impersonal, postulating generalities that could hold for anyone:

Non giova vivere	It is no use living in
orgogliosamente	grand disdain
Qui tutti verranno in umiltà	Here all will come humbly

Finally, there are those that consist of a quotation, often from the Bible or some Church Father:

Non l'abbiamo perduto	We have not lost him
Egli dimora prima	He lives on before us in the
di noi nella luce di Dio	light of God
Santo'Agostino	Saint Augustine

At the end of my notebook are appendixes, where I jot down not whole epitaphs but only the thematic parts. In the first appendix descriptions of graven images, in the second causes of death, in the third the characteristics of the deceased. But the pickings are not rich, ever since cemeteries turned into photograph albums – photos are objective, demonstrating without requiring judgement, setting nobody on edge. No, there's little point in seeking epitaphs in country graveyards these days. Nonetheless, I've always felt at home in these parts, and I think that if one is born in the provinces one should not feel obliged to go anywhere at all, since everything – or almost everything – is already there. I often bump into foreigners who are visiting my region, confirming my idea that there must indeed be a reason to come here (and not to leave).

This is how, near Canossa, I came to know an American architect who was born in Connecticut, who had studied in New Haven, who was living in Illinois, and who had not the slightest idea of where he would die. I became good friends with this American architect, which doubtless explains why I let myself be persuaded to take a plane for the first time in my life and pay him a visit in Vermont, where he has a family home.

In Vermont, I found, there is an awful lot of wood. It's a bit like being at the foot of the Apennines, except there's nobody there, just a few low, unobtrusive, wooden houses. And there are no fences either, so anyone can wander at will. Since there are no fences, there is also an absence of automatic gates; an absence, too, I suppose, of burglar-alarms.

Near the centre of Vermont there is a town that my architect friend wished me to visit since, given its high percentage of inhabitants of Italian origin, he thought it might relieve me of my homesickness. In Barre, Vermont, many years ago, hundreds of Italian families arrived to work in the granite quarries. It's almost like being in Carrara, except that the quarries, instead of being on the mountainside, are on the plain, and instead of being white, are grey. The Barre cemetery exudes an air of tranquillity: a lawn, carefully tended and trimmed; maples, oaks, firs, a few alders shaped like cypresses; a pond with a small bridge; squirrels, brightly coloured birds, tortoises, deer, the occasional racoon.

All the tombs are fashioned out of grey granite. There are none of what I've called 'condominiums' – those walls of burial niches – but lots of steles of various forms and dimensions, plenty of American flags to indicate who among the dead fell in battle, and an almost complete lack of crosses. On the steles are visible only some light ornamental motifs carved into the granite: a sprig of vines, a funerary urn, a Greek fret. Then a series of Italian names: Bardassi, Bedia, Bettini, Brusa, Carmolli, Corti, Ellero, Novelli, Rusconi, Tomasi; the names of stonecutters, dead for the most part of silicosis.

But there are also many tombs on which the stonemasons have sought to defy the intractability of granite. Certain of them are veritable sculptures, of a sort I'd never have expected to see in a cemetery, such as the rally automobile, 'Number 61', belonging to Arman J. Laguerre (born 6.10.1963, died 2.2.1991); or the biplane of Mark Willets (4.4.1911 – 6.3.1936); or the settee in the Frau style, this one too in lifelike proportions, belonging to Tom Teinstein (12.5.1924 – 3.7.1986); or the nuptial bed of Mike and Cathy Oldcorn, depicting the deceased couple hand in hand. Davis, a thirteen-year-old boy, is buried under an enormous granite football.

Here and there the odd epitaph, among which the most essential and touching, also because it was in Italian:

Belli	Belli
Anarchico	Anarchist
m. 11.7.1903	d. 11.7.1903

I lingered, contemplating this inscription, for quite some while. Is it indeed an epitaph? Would it be appropriate for my notebook? If so, in which subcategory would it fit? Had Belli wanted it so, or was this his relatives' choice? The stone was rectangular, very small. Belli, a stonecutter, who had come all the way to Barre, Vermont, to start some revolution or other, then died at some undefined age, with granite dust in his lungs and his native language on his lips. I sensed that Belli, who had passed away without leaving anything but this shortest of epitaphs, might at any moment rise from the grave, as far as his waist, and ask me, with a disdain worthy of Dante's Farinata, what ever had become of his revolutionary campaigns and his political enemies.

For my part, I started coughing and staring silently at my shoes, then distancing myself – all the way to Chicago, where my architect friend currently lives and works.

So now it's Sunday, I'm in Chicago, and it's snowing.

I woke up this morning, I went to the shops, and I found that on Sunday mornings it's not possible to buy alcohol.

'But this is non-alcoholic beer,' I said to the cashier.

'I'm sorry,' she said, 'but before eleven I can't sell anything from the alcohol counter.'

I trudged home under the falling snow, my mind teeming with questions: Would the ban be in operation only on Sundays or on every other day too? Why should non-alcoholic beer be sold from the alcohol counter? Is non-alcoholic beer an oxymoron? Is this the case only at Dominick's? And then, why before eleven? What happens in America after 11 a.m.?

Yesterday evening towards eight I went to Dino's, the other grocery store near the house, to buy milk. On the walk home I saw a group of youngsters enter a house carrying cans of Miller beer. Then I crossed paths with three older men and a woman who were chatting away merrily, each carrying a pack holding eight bottles of beer. I with my gallon of milk, and they with their eight-packs of beer: united in advancing age and in suffering from the cold.

Perhaps, since everyone here tends to get drunk on Saturday nights, the Illinois legislators decided to impose a moratorium on the consumption of alcohol on Sunday mornings? Such was my hypothesis. To get a more reliable explanation I asked Malcolm, my American friend, and discovered that it's only on Sunday mornings before eleven that alcohol cannot be bought, and for the reason that these are the blue hours.

'Yet another expression with the word blue! What is it with that word?'

Malcolm did not follow me: he was not to know I had just finished reading *On Being Blue: A Philosophical Enquiry* by William Gass, a book I had been given so I could judge if I thought it could be translated into Italian. I'd read it out of curiosity but also from a translator's angle, drawing a blank as I did so. Firstly, it was difficult, and secondly, it constantly played upon the double, triple,

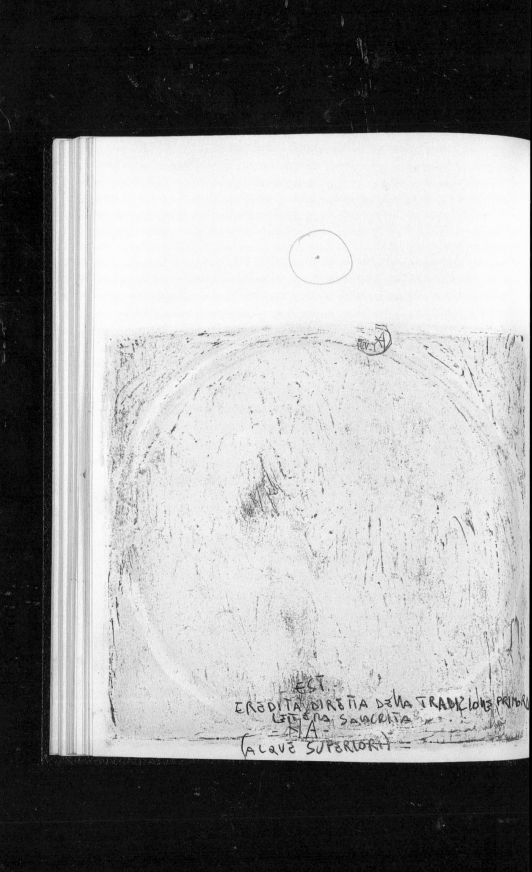

EST.
EREDITA DIRETTA DELLA TRADIZIONE PRIMORD
LETTERA SANCRITA
HA
(ALQUE SUPERIORA)

quadruple significance of that colour. Translating a book like this into Italian would be sure to induce melancholy: a malady that takes hold of you whenever, after a thousand false starts, you feel yourself being invested by an overwhelming sense of inadequacy and impotence. This blue-tinged malady makes the translator wish that Babel and the multiplication of languages were only a legend, and that all the various languages in the world did not exist and had never existed. With melancholy comes nostalgia for an ur-language, in which colours and all their meanings were the same for everyone, in which plants were identical for all and sundry; in which flowers, and sounds, and ceremonies, every object, sensation, and belief was expressed in a single, universal, manner, in which a rose was a rose was a rose.

But alas, the multiplication of languages is no fairy-tale, and in English the word *blue* has come to signify many things, among which sadness and melancholy, which are expressed in other ways and by other colours for an Italian. *True blue, bluenose, blue Communist, blue water, blue law, blue counties, bluestocking, blue ribbon*... Not to repeat it ad nauseam (or until I'm *blue in the face*), English and Italian do not share many expressions when it comes to colour. Feeling blue gives *umor nero*, meaning a black mood, not a blue. Perhaps the most curious difference relates to cinema: Why in Italian are pornographic movies *red* whereas in English they are (or were) *blue*? Experts do appear to agree that there exists a close relation between sexual activity and the colour blue – an archetypal relation that stretches across cultures. The Chinese, for instance, tint the walls of their brothels blue. The colour of Satan's sulphurous flame is blue for Americans. Blue was the puritanical pencil used in the nineteenth century by the public censor when prohibiting printed matter unsuited to the eyes of the innocent...

This thought of blue pencils puts me in mind of how, when I was at school, errors marked in blue were more serious than those marked in red. In translations from Latin, for example, the blue errors subtracted one point, those in red only half a point. It always seemed to me it should be the other way round: in my mind red was the colour of maximum error (one didn't cross a red traffic-light, one didn't enter a cinema projecting red movies, and one didn't visit Communist-run workers' centres with their red flags at their entrances, and which, according to the curate instructing us in catechism, were strictly out of bounds); while blue seemed more neutral, closer to the azure of the national football team, to the veil of the Madonna, or to *Pinocchio*'s Fairy with Turquoise Hair. But of course the teachers were right: blue minus one point, red minus half a point.

Yesterday evening, *out of the blue*, after thinking about all those folk in the snow with their crates of beer, I got to feeling like a drink. So I parked the milk in the fridge, and set off for Buddy Guy's Legends, on Wabash. Even if it is a rather mournful dive, decked out for European tourists in search of authentic blues, one can still sit quietly in a corner and listen to some excellent music. Last night, there was a young local group whose song, 'The First Time I Met the Blues', reminded me of how the blues can become a sort of demon taking possession of the musicians. The blues don't get made by those who are light of heart. The blues are piercing and lacerating, like the arrows of love in the poetry of Guido Cavalcanti. There's a physical battle between the palpable melancholy that propagates, pursues, paralyses, and the musician who attempts to flee but succumbs. This is a hunt that repeats, rhythmically, with defined cadences and structure, following symmetrical patterns (the blues' famous twelve bars) with their three-line stanzas in which the words of the second line echo those of the first and prepare those of the third which close the circle in a rhyme, but always in movement, as if the hunt were never done, as if nothing could ever be definitive – and this from the outset with the notes themselves, the blue notes that are a dissonant particularity of this type of music.

While listening, I was struck by how our usual necessities and nostalgias, our cultures and habits, when they seek expression, oblige us to invent new and beautiful and disturbing forms. It is said that *blue notes* were first heard in the voices of black slaves stooped in labour, then in guitars played with bottle-necks, then in harmonicas played a little out of tune. These are half-way between the notes to which Western traditions of refined music have accustomed us. Nearly all our instruments are manufactured so that the interval between one note and another, between one semitone and another, should be precise. Similarly, our musical scales are composed of twelve semitones, where African scales are often pentatonic, with different intervals. And this is so, when trying to obtain a certain note on an instrument conceived for different notes is rather like trying to translate the *Divina Commedia* into English, or *Hamlet* into Italian. Those African singers who tried to celebrate their gods, mixing their own musical cultures and adapting these to Western instruments, effected a translation, an adaptation which permitted them to keep alive (or revive) their own musical sensibilities and cultures, in a musical creole – a fruitful contamination. If in the blues C major is the principal chord, blue notes correspond to the third, fifth, or seventh note in the major scale lowered not by a semitone, but sung or played slightly flatter, or lower in pitch than is correct by Western standards. Not only, therefore, an E flat in the place of an E, but rather a somewhat declining E flat, on which the slide guitar or harmonica lingers, dipping our ears towards a different sonority. This may amount to a non-standard note, or even an ungainly note, yet it is the miracle of such a translation that it succeeds in making audible the melancholy and nostalgia of a lost language of sound, the language of a violently extirpated African musicality.

As I made my way home from Buddy Guy's Legends, under the snow that had not ceased falling, I thought to myself: Could it be that any translation, if it seeks to be more than a cold and sterile transposition, must contain blue notes? A translation needs blue notes to hint at an elsewhere, at nostalgia, and with nostalgia the tension provoked by unappeased desire for whatever is distant and unreachable. As William Gass puts it, 'So it's true: Being without being is blue.'

I was fortunate enough to hear him – not Gass, but another great American writer – for the first time at a poetry-reading in Chicago. Then I learned that he was looking for someone to give him Italian lessons. For me, it was a chance not to be missed, and I promptly presented myself at his office, on the fourth floor of a small gothic edifice that was covered in ivy (as buildings really ought to be in top American universities). Such corridors always make me feel shy and awkward; and I felt even more shy and awkward when I knocked.

Paul Laconam, Poet Laureate of the American Congress, was very tall and thin, with a lined face, but was still youthful in his elegant demeanour. He was also polite, thanking me for making myself available. We decided to meet once a week, over his lunch hour, to chat in Italian. He knew the language, had translated Dante into English, but wanted regular practice.

For me, this weekly meeting was a goldmine. Since I sought nothing in exchange, Paul Laconam offered me, as reward for my availability, his several volumes of verse. (I believe he did so out of generosity, but also a little out of vanity – such vanity as poets frequently display.) Since the best way of reading a book, as Italo Calvino used to say (and as many said before him), is to translate it, I tried to translate him – the better to read and understand him. After our weekly meetings, I had the privilege of asking him directly, as a poet, if my translation was on track, if it was succeeding in not betraying his intention. He would correct me when I went obviously astray, but he never said anything when my version interpreted a phrase in a manner that was legitimate linguistically but not what he had intended. We would lose ourselves in long discussions of the sense of his lines; one time he admitted that he no longer remembered why he had written a certain very ambiguous line, and that it seemed to him my interpretation was more convincing than his own.

Gradually, I managed to get through a fair old stack of Paul Laconam's poems, translated for the pleasure of reading them optimally. Then, since translators, in their own way, are just as vain as poets, I asked if he'd be willing to let me publish my translations. I say *vain* because everyone knows that there's no money to be made in translating poetry, and that the only return, beyond the personal pleasure of winning some sort of competition with the source text, is that of seeing one's name printed on the cover – even if only as the author's chauffeur (or little more than this). Paul Laconam consented enthusiastically, and so I started searching for, and then found, an Italian publisher.

The project looked about to come off, when an unforeseen difficulty appeared on the horizon, in the person of the poet's True Italian Translator (who for discretion's sake I shall call 'Signor Vetri' – Mr Glass). When Signor Vetri got wind of the fact that His Poet was about to be published in Italian by some unknown translator who had met the master only by chance, who had not shared (as he had done) an intense correspondence with the Poet, who had published not a single translation or essay on the Poet, in short one who displayed no elective affinity or consanguinity with the great Paul Laconam – as I say, when Signor Vetri learned of this project, he bared his teeth and nails, and, like a lover betrayed, wrote the Poet a letter full of passionate resentment. In his letter Signor Vetri stacked the arguments as to why the Poet should review his decision and not confide his poetic word to an upstart interpreter. One line of argument was psychological and sought leverage in feelings, citing the personal dedication of Vetri over time. Another was deontological, and cited the fact that nobody had ever doubted his professionalism or competence, especially as his own translations had obeyed the criterion of maximal faithfulness to the original (as various reviews had underlined). But the principal argument, sustained by quotations from a major Italian intellectual (Director of a highly influential literary review and a friend of his), was pragmatic: it claimed that a foreign poet, once he has found in a new language a voice that permits him to speak to the hearts of a new audience, should not alter it, the risk being that of a radical loss of identity. From the outset, Signor Vetri had been the Italian voice of the Poet, and any alternative voice would merely alienate the ears of the Poet's readers. How could they recognise the tones, nuances, and rhythms if these had not been transported by the voice of Signor Vetri?

It would be as if Hardy (of Laurel and Hardy) were no longer to speak in the voice of Alberto Sordi, his famous Italian dubber, but in that of, say, Marcello Mastroianni. (The Laurel and Hardy case did not feature in Signor Vetri's letter, needless to say, which would never have stooped to such an example.) The fact that in English Hardy might be a tenor and not a bass (as he becomes in Sordi's dubbing), with an accent from the deep south of the United States, and Laurel might have a British accent and thus be linguistically light years away from his partner, was insignificant: in Italian, Laurel and Hardy (Stanlio e Ollio) have the selfsame accent, the one that an Anglophone is likely to have when speaking Italian (or the one that a Roman actor has when imitating an American speaking Italian). And that's all that matters!

In order to avoid provoking dangerous identity crises and jealous scenes, I stepped aside and withdrew my project. Yet I did continue to wonder what might have happened had Paul Laconam disembarked in Italy with a modified voice. There might then have been two Paul Laconams, just as there are dozens of Catulluses, Sapphos, Aristophaneses, all roaming together round our country as they have done for centuries; dozens of versions of the body of the same writer, each with a different voice. After visiting homes, schools, theatres, and universities, these variously-voiced bodies presumably find themselves alongside one another in alphabetical order on our library shelves. Homer sings the gesture of Achilles at the opening of *The Iliad* modulated in the rhyming octets of the Jesuit Giuseppe Bozoli (1769-1770), which were followed by the hendecasyllables of Vincenzo Monti (1810), which of course preceded the free verse version by Rosa Calzecchi Onesti (1963), which was succeeded by the prose attempt by Maria Grazia Ciani (1990), and so on... One can only imagine the squabbles and jealous scenes: 'Homer's mine, and mine alone.' 'No, I'm the only one who really understands him.' 'It's me who speaks for him, who ignites his verse.' 'Impostor!' 'Traitor!' 'Translator...'

Of a night, there must be quite some turbulence in the library stacks, what with all those competing voices. And it's clear that the music does indeed change according to who is playing – and just as well, too: what a bore it would be to hear over and over Beethoven's 'Eroica' Symphony in the way it was played in public the first time, on 7 April 1805 in the Theater an der Wien. To translate is to betray – *tradurre è tradire* – and only through betrayal is a writer's voice kept alive. To the liveliness of this voice in time will correspond the number of voices multiplying it, so permitting it to dialogue across the ages. At root, even a simple phrase with which a sentiment or a thought or a concept seeks to express itself *translates* this sentiment, this thought, this concept, in the very moment it vibrates through the air. There are 'never enough words, never enough words,' as the poet Mariangela Gualtieri has said. And words may be the most vital gift we can offer, even if they are imperfect, approximate, or a tad reductive.

It is curious indeed that some translators still swear by fidelity. There is no real fidelity when it comes to translation, just as there is no real fidelity in any sort of words. At most, texts can be

- PIANTA -

4

transported in a purposeful manner, with seriousness or daring, and a frank avowal of what the intention was in translating, of what has been lost, and of what gained if and when the inevitable losses have found compensation. Yet there is still betrayal. The fidelity of the translator to the author is akin to the fidelity of the author to the translator, or to that sworn between two lovers: for Catullus, the fidelity sworn by a woman to 'a passionate lover' was 'written in the wind and the running water'. In the context of translation, the word 'fidelity' may end up being synonymous with a lack of judgement and common sense, even with hypocrisy.

I continued to visit Paul Laconam, but between us there never arose another translation: rather, a discreet, decorous, strictly monolingual conversation.

On that typical Chicago street named Michigan Avenue, I was certain not to meet anyone I knew, and I was being very careful where I placed my feet – not that there was much to see in any case: skyscrapers in every style, contemporary sculptures, flowerbeds, and a multitude of windows. Though I'd never been here before, everything seemed to me just as it should be and as I'd have predicted. Everything was so orderly and well laid out as to seem counterfeit: the white buses with their red and blue stripes, the yellow taxis, the passers-by on rollerblades who were darting between pedestrians and cars, the woman with the elegant flowery suit, the sax player on the corner, the traffic-cops with their powerful physiques and ample gestures, like those of consummate actors or lunatics let out for a day. Everything as it should have been.

When I then watched this counterfeit reflected in the vast windows of the skyscrapers, I felt like I was at the movies. On the other side of the smoked glass, someone else, invisible to me, might have been wondering what on earth I was staring at: I was watching the world passing behind my back with the gaze of a cinema-goer who is hoping to be enchanted. In those cinematographic images I would occasionally observe someone who, like me, was staring at something unidentifiable, on foot in the middle of the sidewalk, with the cars passing behind him. Of course, that something was me. But how did I get myself cast in this movie? This was nothing like the times when I'd caught a glimpse of myself in the shop windows of the Via Emilia back home. The sight of myself reflected on those Michigan Avenue screens constrained me to lower my gaze and to set off again, taking care not to trip myself up, suddenly realising that it was obvious I was there by chance, that I did not belong, that I hadn't grasped the basics of life here – and it showed.

I spoke of this to Malcolm, my architect friend and host, and he gifted me a slim volume from his library, published in 1880: 10.5 x 13.6 centimetres, 96 pages, costing one shilling sterling, entitled *Don't: A Manual of Mistakes & Improprieties More or Less Prevalent in Conduct and Speech*. It was his way, characteristically pragmatic and discreet, of helping me comprehend where I was. This book comprises a series of precepts that all begin with 'Don't': what not to do on the road, at table, in the drawing-room, in the shops. Here are a few precepts that served to remind me of why it was all too obvious on Michigan Avenue that I was an Italian and not a local: 'Don't neglect to keep to the right of the promenade, otherwise there may be collisions and much confusion.' 'Don't stare at people, or laugh at any peculiarity of manner or dress. Don't point at persons or objects. Don't turn and look after people that have passed.' These interdictions fly in the face of every norm of Italian sociability. 'Don't obstruct the entrance to churches, theatres, or assemblies. Don't stand before hotels or other places and stare at passers-by.' What is the point of public assembly, in Italy, if not to stop and stare? 'Don't rush for a seat in a car or at a public entertainment, in utter disregard of every one else, pushing rudely by women and children, hustling men who are older or less active, and disregarding every law of politeness.'

And I've seen these precepts applied with my very own eyes, for instance at Sunday sporting gatherings. To the east of Chicago, between the highway and Lake Michigan, for several kilometres there stretches a park that serves as a sort of elongated piazza and lung for the city. In the middle of this park are two asphalt tracks: one reserved for pedestrians, the other for cyclists. During the weekends these transform into torrential rivers of sports enthusiasts: old men running, middle-aged men and women jogging with weights round their ankles and wrists, youngsters on rollerblades wearing knee-pads and helmets, young women in gym-shoes with dogs on leashes, parents pushing snoozing babies in streamlined strollers as they run; all heading determinedly forward on the right, paying no attention to whoever is racing along beside them. Then turning and heading back in the opposite direction.

This very orderly way of proceeding, of obeying precepts, is apparently in the blood. But for precepts firmly to take root, the basics have to be grasped young. So it was that on summer afternoons I'd watch hundreds of children playing football on the pitches beside the lake, each with his own leather ball, shin-guards, and brand-new soccer strip. They trot round skittles set out by a trainer with whistle and cap. As they imbibe the lesson, their parents watch proudly from behind a fence. Behind a different fence, other parents are watching other children get to grips with the basics of baseball. Then there's American football, volleyball, rugby. The one thing I never saw was a squad of young cyclists, as I regularly do back home. Could it be that cycling requires no basic precepts, being a matter of just climbing onto one's bike, finding one's balance, then pushing off and pedalling?

In Chicago, the favourite sport after baseball, especially on summer evenings at the weekend, is the barbecue, as becomes clear from the odour of charred meat that creeps over the city towards dusk. As distinct from all the other activities, which these days are shared between men and women alike, preparation of the grill is the unique preserve of men. When it comes to the cooking, very little is left to the eye or to chance. There are charts for times and temperatures and every sort of thermometer (inside and outside the grill, and another with a sensitive nozzle that gets inserted into the meat to measure its innermost temperature). Naturally, there is some degree of flexibility, otherwise there'd be no sense to the long discussions of the best way to prepare the food, discussions that constitute the opening salvo of every festa.

One has barely arrived before a bottle of ice-cold beer is thrust into one's hand, with no accompanying glass. Approaching the grill, one can see the host at work with his weaponry of tongs and wire brushes. Brief introductions before the discussion turns to the meat, which in the meantime has begun to change colour over the glowing charcoal. Despite my always having a dictionary to hand, I never managed to get far in such conversations, because of my complete lack of grounding in the basics. But parties where one is on one's feet offer an easy escape route: hardly has a discussion begun to languish before one changes places, employing any banal excuse (another bottle of beer?) – and so begins a new discussion with some new person or other.

The advantage of being Italian at such parties is that practically every conversation runs along predictable lines; and this, for a foreigner who hasn't yet mastered the language, is a real advantage. It feels much like repeating those dialogues learned by heart in English-language textbooks, where there's no requirement to try to be original. One quickly discovers that all the other party guests have been to Italy when they were aged between eighteen and twenty-two, that they've visited Rome, Florence, and Venice, that they know a few words of Italian, a little about fashion designers, opera, cuisine, and that they're planning a trip there – in the course of which they may even pay me a visit. At which point there follows the not disinterested question: 'But what city did you say you were from?'

And the standard reply: 'Reggio Emilia, in the north, between Milan and Florence.'

This reply gives rise to several responses, depending on the interlocutor. If it's someone who's especially interested in food, there may follow: 'Reggio Emilio like *Reggiano cheese*?' (this being how true Parmigiano is called over there, to distinguish it from imitations that go by the name of 'Parmesan cheese'). If the interlocutor has a thing for cars, the response may be: 'Reggio Emilia, in the region where they make Ferrari, Maserati, Lamborghini?' Or the response of those easily identified sports fanatics: 'Ah, where Kobe Bryant grew up, when his dad was playing in Italy.'

The verb to *mingle* is much repeated at barbecues. It's employed when it's pretty clear that the conversation is languishing and the bottle of beer is not yet empty. What then follows is 'I don't want to hold you back from *mingling* with the others' – as if mingling were the principal purpose of the gathering, the law conferring upon the group its vital homeostasis. People shift around continually, meet somebody, drink beer, then strike up a conversation with somebody new. One feels at the centre of a square dance where one changes partners frequently

"SUD"

- MANIFESTAZIONE·

in synch with the staccato rhythm of banjo, guitar, and fiddle. By the end of the quadrille, tired and somewhat intoxicated, one has got to know many people and one has also gained confidence in one's linguistic abilities, since there's nothing more reassuring and restful than uttering stock phrases and platitudes.

Dinners in the Italian provinces are, by contrast, more similar to waltzes. You sit at table and does not budge, hour after hour, from *antipasto* to *dolce*, doing the rounds with at most two companions. First you dance with the person seated to your right. Then with the person seated to your left. If the conversation languishes, there is no escape, the waltz has to last right through *caffè*. You remain seated a captive audience for whoever believes – and there's always someone – he has something intelligent to say, and then you go to bed with a sore head, feeling like you have talked to nobody and had hardly any fun at all.

What is true, though, is that such enforced propinquity can have the effect of driving one off the standardised lines of conversation, pushing one out into dangerous terrain. The *Don't* book Malcolm gave me is categorical on this: 'Don't introduce political or religious discussion. Speech on these subjects can easily be the cause of irritation and is therefore better avoided.' Hard to imagine getting through an Italian dinner without such subjects. 'Don't speak of your illnesses or personal afflictions, whatever their type.' But what's the use of Italian hypochondria if not to be talked about? 'Exaggerated praise is nauseating, but on the other hand indiscriminate condemnation is irritating.' 'Don't ever expatiate on results you have achieved or are achieving, nor on your particular abilities.' And finally: 'Listening to everyone attentively is one of the cardinal points in a good education.' Instructions which, if followed to the letter, would spell the demise not just of the Italian dinner party, but of Italian conviviality and family life!

And even if it is decreed in the book of *Don't* that the ability to listen is one of the essential characteristics of an educated person, it's not a given that will-power alone can guarantee this. Sometimes an individual may wish to listen to others but be unable to do so, as if the sense of hearing were being impeded by something physiological. Rosa Turchetti, for example, who when she was small lived next door to me, went on to become immensely wealthy. She became wealthy because, as her sister put it, ever since she was a baby she had a 'strong business sense'. According to her sister, who was my friend and who had looked into the question, there are five normal senses employed in concrete experience: sight, hearing, smell, taste, and touch. Other senses can be added, which vary from country to country and depend on the psychological theory. The sixth sense permits those who have it to predict the future (mothers often have it, and may develop it during pregnancy). The seventh sense is the sense of business, which allows whoever has it to understand immediately if economic advantage can be drawn from any given situation. If it's hard to describe, that's precisely because one has to have it to be able to speak of it, and those who have it are always busy making money – and in any case it's their form of royal prerogative which they have no reason to divulge.

After working for some years in domestic appliances, Rosa felt that this cash-cow was about to dry up. She moved into informatics, profitably, before feeling that this too was set to dry up. Given that she had stashed away a good portion of her gains, she decided to pursue the dream of a market that would never dry up. One day, she scented a powerful odour of cash in contemporary art, an area where the personal capacity of the dealer is of paramount importance – the gallery-owner not only invents the market, but also the artist and the product if she's good at it (and Rosa clearly was).

In the bat of an eyelid, Rosa became a successful gallery-owner, assisted by her seventh sense. But this sense, like most muscles when exercised, became ever more developed. It developed so much that it began to win ground in her brain over the other senses, particularly that of hearing. We realised this during the course of our summer dinners, when she would hold forth, not letting a word in edgewise, never heeding anyone. Even her husband realised it, because when he would call to her softly, she would fail to respond. He obliged her to consult a famous hearing specialist, who immediately had her undergo a CAT scan that revealed how her brain had been invaded by this seventh sense which had completely triumphed over her sense of hearing – and there was no known remedy.

Rosa was not informed of this, so that, unaware of the problem in the first place, she should not be upset. The more her seventh sense grew, and the richer she became, the more impervious she also became to the outside world. The sounds would beat against her eardrums, but she would repulse them without registering a thing. Henceforth, her world was completely silent, not unlike the canvases of many of the artists exhibited in her gallery. But within that great silence, broken only by the sound of her own voice, she felt entirely at ease.

Unlike Myrna – now, she did know how to listen. And with her, the conversation took an unexpected turn.

I was at a back-yard barbecue party in Rogers Park in north Chicago, close to where Malcolm lives. Everything was going normally, with chat and beer. Change your partner. Chat and beer. Change your partner... until the force behind the mingling, the force determining that by the end everyone would have talked to everyone else and that the conversation would have remained resolutely superficial – the force got blocked, and I found myself conversing over and over with Myrna and Myrna alone.

It requires some degree of patience to talk with someone who is stumbling along in a language not his own, and Myrna was amply endowed with this blessed patience. I attempted to say things that strayed from the standardised well-rehearsed lines, but the sentences came out broken and contorted, the words sounding raucous, like chalk screeching down a blackboard. Myrna, with a lovely, simple, curious smile, picked up on my sentences and completed them, repeating them back to me graciously. She brought them out all lined up and musical, with just the tone I would have used myself, had my mouth and my breath ever learned the basics. Myrna was a sort of echo-chamber perfecting my voice. It was like looking in a magic mirror that transformed and beautified the me it reflected. I don't know if she felt the same when I corrected the pronunciation of the few words of Italian she ventured. Yet I almost immediately had the feeling that some sort of exchange was beginning to happen between us. I certainly listened to myself in her, and I was managing also to look her straight in the eyes without feeling like I was importuning her.

When, the following day, I saw our reflection in the window of a shop on Michigan Avenue, with the world passing by behind us, I still did not lower my gaze: I was beginning to feel a little bit at home.

After several trips to and fro across the Atlantic, and after much navigation of English-Italian dictionaries, I eventually settled back down in Reggio Emilia. Lest my prophecy not be fulfilled, that I should die in the province where I was born, I decided to consign my passport to the back of a drawer and calmly wait to see what might happen next.

One day, returning from one of my little bicycle tours in the Apennines, what should I find in my postbox but a large yellow envelope, sent from France, covered in postage stamps. Inside the envelope was a handwritten letter and some thirty-odd typewritten pages in English. The letter was signed by a Scottish translator who, he told me, had come across a copy of *La malinconia del traduttore*, my book of highly personal essays about my travels and translations. Having read it, he had decided to translate it, and, if I was in agreement, to publish it in the series of chapbooks of which he was the editor; only, he explained to me, he would be obliged to cut it down to one fifth of its original length since that was all that there would be room for. If it was all right with me, he would like to call his pared-down version of my essays *Translator's Blues*. He said that he had tried to give my text a new look, bearing in mind not only the English language but also the expectations of the readers of the series he edited.

Taken aback by such a gesture, I found myself wanting to thank this Scottish translator straight off, even before I had started in on his translation. It's not that I'm so generous or undiscerning, but that I had developed a theory, a theory which said that authors were all too inclined to interfere in the translation of their own books. My theory was part and parcel of my overview of life, an overview that might best be called a philosophy of vanishing: get yourself as little noticed as possible, stow away your passport, leave things to take care of themselves, and leave whatever has to happen to . . . well, happen.

When Umberto Eco brought out his book called *Dire quasi la stessa cosa* (*Saying almost the same thing* – a wonderful title for a book on translation), I remember thinking that this was an example of the exact opposite of my philosophy of vanishing.

Eco's position seemed to me Ecocentric, as for him the intention of the author had decidedly to prevail over the intention of the translator – over the text itself, if needs be. Eco dwelt at length on the translations of his own bestseller *The Name of the Rose*, on his relations with his translators, and on his attempts to rein in interpretations he judged too free; he did so quite as if he had never been the author of that important book of literary theory entitled *Opera aperta* (*The Open Work*). The same was true of Douglas Hofstadter, who, like Eco, had written lots of wise things about translation theory: none of which prevented him from issuing very precise instructions to his translators, larded with abundant examples from his masterpiece *Gödel, Escher, Bach*.

For me, the position of Eco and Hofstadter towards their translators was presumptuous and high-handed. For me, following my theory, a book should be like a son or a daughter: having produced a child, the author needs to accept that it will grow up, be free to wander, to choose its own political positions, a different career, to find a companion capable of listening to it and smoothing out its words (as Myrna had listened to and corrected mine) – even if this companion would not be the one that the author-father might have chosen. No meddling! Such was the quasi-Buddhist motto I thought to apply to the translation of my own work. There had been more than enough meddling when it came to giving life to the child in the first place; now that she was born and raised, her life was hers to live, her relations were her own to develop.

That was my theory, and that is what I intended to write to the Scottish translator without even dipping into his translation. But then curiosity got the better of me: I succumbed to the wish to see how what had once been my text – mine and mine alone – had changed. As I read, it was like seeing a child who, unannounced, has just returned home after several long years in some far-off land. He was unrecognisable when he opened the front door.

I was paralysed, thrown into a strange gloom or despondency filled with melancholic musing. Who are you?

On closer inspection, through some strange alchemy, the familiar features began to make themselves known: what was becoming discernible, not without a surge of nostalgia, was the unforgettable face of the infant; it was palpable within the lineaments of the now mature face of the grown-up who, by maturing and ageing, looked even more like the father than before – or indeed, like the father's father.

In Italian, the word for constraints (as in a 'translation constraint') is *vincoli*. But this word is also used to indicate the family bonds that tie together generations of relatives. Children, parents, grandparents...they all move, have reasons for shifting, for running around in time and space, back and forth, from one continent to another, from one language to another – sometimes limiting their movements to within the same dull province. They are individuals, autonomous voices, certainly, yet they are oddly chained and restricted by their familial bonds, by their *vincoli*: indeed, it is because of these very *vincoli* that they are what they are.

COLOPHON

THE CAHIERS SERIES · NUMBER 26
ISBN: 978-1-90963111-3

Printed by Principal Colour, Paddock Wood, on
Neptune Unique (text) and Chagall (dust jacket).
Set in Giovanni Mardersteig's Monotype Dante.

Series Editor: Dan Gunn
Associate Series Editor: Daniel Medin
Design: Sylph Editions Design

Text: ©Franco Nasi, 2015
Images: © Massimo Antonaci, *Drawings* 1991-1995
Photos: © Dario Lasagni, 2015

With thanks to Marie Donnelly, and to the Tides
Foundation, for their generous support.

CENTER FOR WRITERS & TRANSLATORS
THE AMERICAN UNIVERSITY OF PARIS

SYLPH EDITIONS, LONDON | 2015

THE AMERICAN
UNIVERSITY 50
of PARIS YEARS

center for writers and translators

SYLPH
EDITIONS

www.aup.edu · www.sylpheditions.com

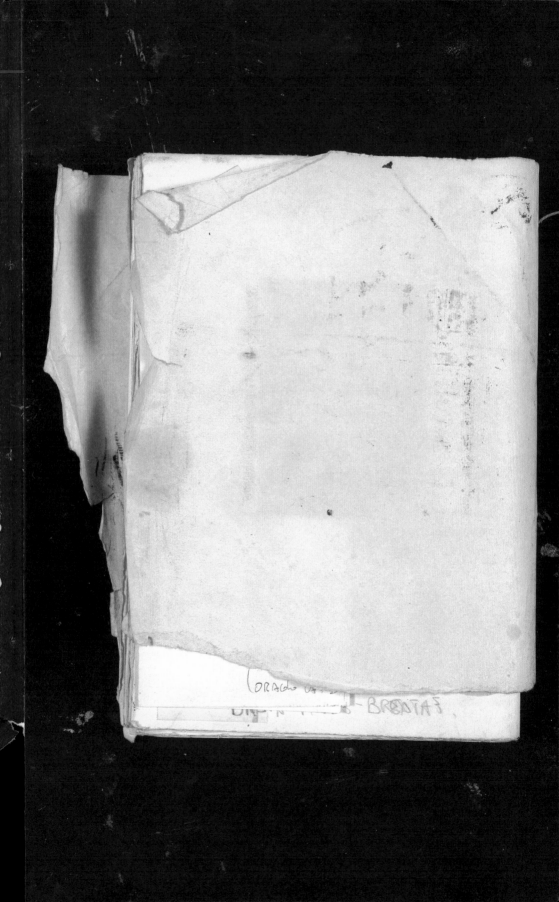

CORACÃO DE ... BREATA?